The
Time Web

Written by Roderick Hunt
and illustrated by Alex Brychta

OXFORD
UNIVERSITY PRESS

Before reading

- Read the back cover text and page 4. Why do you think Biff and Chip are so anxious?
- Look at page 5. What are the four parts of the TimeWeb?

After reading

- Would you rather go into the past or the future? If the future, what would you like to see or find out?

Book quiz

1 Which part of the TimeWeb does Neena bring back?
  a The Cell
  b The Hub
  c The Matrix
2 What happens to make the Circularium start working again?
3 Where did Biff and Chip travel to?

See p45 for the book quiz answers!

The story so far ...

Virans are a virus spreading through time.
Their purpose is to bring about chaos and
darkness by destroying history as we know it.
Mortlock, the Time Guardian, has one last
hope of defeating the Virans – the TimeWeb.
Can the children go back in time, recover
the parts of the TimeWeb and return safely?
Or will the mission be too difficult and
dangerous?

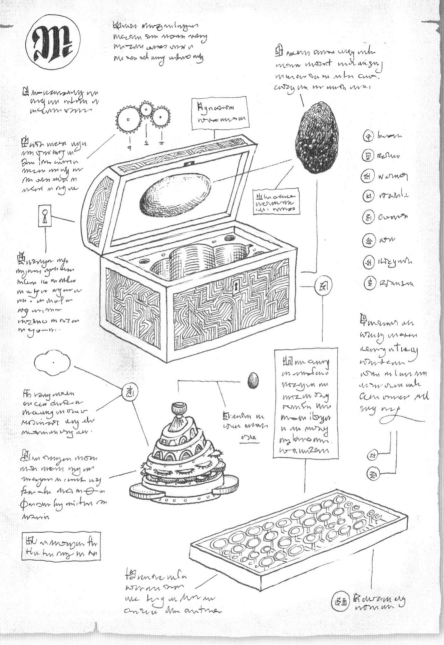

The Parts of the TimeWeb

"The TimeWeb is an ancient machine. It acts like an eye looking into the past ... See, it has four parts. The Hub ... the Matrix ... the Cell ... and the box is the case which connects it all together."

Theodore Mortlock – Time Guardian

Chapter 1

Biff and Chip waited anxiously in the
Circularium. Chip kept looking at the
doors through which the others had vanished
only moments earlier.

Biff stared at the hourglass. She watched
the last few specks of light flowing down.
Would everyone return safely? She held
her breath.

Mortlock had not moved, but as the last specks of light slipped into the lower part of the hourglass he let out a deep sigh.

From beneath them came a deep rumbling sound, as if a heavy machine was working. The Circularium began to spin. Once again, the doors seemed to merge into one.

Then Wilf appeared. He was holding a small but highly intricate machine made of polished metal. It had tiny gold wheels and cogs, springs and coils of silver wire, and parts made of glass and crystal. In the very centre was a large sapphire of the deepest blue.

Wilf smiled broadly. "I've got the Hub!" he said excitedly. "The TimeWeb's hard drive!"

Next to appear was Neena. She was holding a metal tray. It was like a keyboard with strange and beautiful symbols. Neena held it carefully as if afraid to drop it.

"The Matrix," she said. "I had a scary time bringing it back."

The Circularium spun again. Wilma and Nadim were flung out of it.

"Virans were after us," panted Nadim. "We just got away in time."

Wilma held a large lump of dark metal. It was the Cell.

The rumbling under the floor stopped. The three open doors round the edge of the room closed gently. The Circularium had shut down. All was so quiet, the children could almost hear the dust settling.

Then Biff broke the silence. Her voice rose in panic. "Where's Kipper?" she shouted. "Why hasn't he come back?"

Chapter 2

Nadim looked startled. He spun round, expecting Kipper to be behind him.

"Things got tricky," he said. "We were running away from the Viran ..."

"Kipper ran back," gasped Wilma. "He ran back to help that boy called Tyler. I'm sorry. I should have stopped him."

Chip turned to Mortlock. "We must rescue Kipper," he said urgently. "How do we go back to find him?"

Mortlock frowned. "The Circularium has stopped. We'll try using the TimeWeb."

He lay the box on the floor and opened the lid. Then he took the Hub from Wilf. It slid perfectly into place. He put the Matrix some distance from it.

"Now, Wilma!" he said. "Put the Cell in the lid of the box. It will power the TimeWeb up. The sapphire will glow, then a web of light will form above it."

Wilma did as Mortlock asked, but nothing happened. Mortlock tapped some symbols on the Matrix, but still the jewel did not glow.

"It's not working," said Nadim.

Chapter 3

"Why isn't it working?" shouted Biff. "Kipper's in danger. What if he can't get back? What if the Virans have got him?"

At that moment, one of the doors in the Circularium began to open.

"Is it Kipper?" asked Neena.

But it wasn't Kipper. It was Floppy. He had found his way down from the library.

When Floppy saw the children he rushed towards them.

"Floppy!" shouted Wilf.

In his excitement, Floppy crashed into the hourglass, toppling it over. Then he leapt up at Chip with his tail wagging.

Mortlock dived towards the hourglass and grabbed it, just before it hit the floor.

As it fell, a few specks of light flowed upwards. As Mortlock set it upright, the bright specks began to trickle down again.

A rumbling came from below the floor. The Circularium had begun to work once more.

Chapter 4

Kipper appeared, but he was not alone.
"Kipper!" shouted Biff.

"And Tyler!" exclaimed Wilma. "How did
you escape? I was sure that Viran was going
to get you."

Tyler gave a cheeky grin. "It was thanks to Kipper," he said. "I rammed my wheelchair into the Viran. As the Viran jumped aside, 'e got too close to a printing press. So Kipper pulled this lever and trapped his coat tail."

"Then the door appeared," said Kipper, "so here we are."

Floppy woofed and ran to greet Kipper.

"When the hourglass fell over, the Circularium worked again," said Mortlock.

"A good job too," said Wilma, "or Kipper and Tyler might still be in the clutches of those Virans. But the Circularium seems to have a mind of its own. I don't get it."

"Hmm!" sniffed Mortlock. "It's an ancient time-travel machine and not reliable! But now we have the TimeWeb! It will detect the past precisely, and you can travel to an exact time in history quite safely."

The TimeWeb was still on the floor where Mortlock had set it up.

Tyler looked at it. "Is this the TimeWeb?" he asked. "It ain't very big."

"It doesn't work," said Nadim. "Even though it's connected up."

"Hang on," said Tyler. "Has the box got a keyhole? Maybe it needs a key."

Mortlock slapped his forehead. "What a fool I am," he said. "Biff and Chip have the key. They've been keeping it!"

Everyone looked at Biff.

"Oh no!" she said. "It's in my sock drawer back at home."

"We could go home and get it," said Kipper. "We don't live far away."

"We're inside a fold in time," said Mortlock. "Getting out is quite easy. But getting back again will be difficult."

"But if we need the key ..." said Chip.

Suddenly the hourglass began to move by itself. It turned once, then it turned again. The grains of light began to flow upwards.

Once more, a rumbling began beneath the floor of the Circularium.

"What's going on?" gasped Chip.

"This is most unusual!" said Mortlock.
"The Circularium is sending somebody
out again. It must be you, Biff and Chip. It
wants you to get the key."

"But why is the hourglass working upside
down?" asked Biff.

"You will be sent forward in time – into the future. So you must not be seen, not by anyone. Remember! Do not be seen!"

The Circularium began to spin. Then all went quiet.

This time, Biff and Chip had vanished.

Chapter 5

B iff and Chip were standing in their own
back garden. It was dark but every light in
the house was blazing.

The back door opened. Dad came out and
went to the bottom of the garden.

Biff and Chip ducked behind the shed.

Dad had a party hat on and he was carrying
a large firework.

"Only three minutes to go," called Dad, going back inside.

"I bet it's New Year's Eve," said Chip. "Dad will let that firework off just after midnight. So we must get the key before he comes back."

Suddenly, Mum came to the window. Biff and Chip gasped.

Through the window they saw themselves.
Kipper was there, and so were Wilf and
Wilma and their mum and dad.

They were all wearing party hats.

"Weird!" gasped Chip. "It's like seeing a
film with us in it. No wonder Mortlock told
us not to let anyone see us!"

"Stay here," said Biff. "I'll get the key. Now is the best time."

She ran across the lawn and crept into the house. Chip closed his eyes. He heard voices calling, "Happy New Year!"

"Hurry up, Biff!" he whispered. "What's taking you so long?"

Chip waited, but Biff didn't appear.

Dad came down the garden again. Chip
crouched behind the shed. Dad lit the
firework and ran back to the house.

"Whoossssh!" The firework lit up the sky.
In seconds it was all over.

Then Biff appeared at the top of the fence
and dropped down beside him.

"I was getting worried," hissed Chip.

"I got the key, but I almost bumped into Mum. I went out the front and ran down next door's garden. No one saw me," said Biff.

A blue door appeared in the fence.

At that moment, Dad rushed down the garden with a bucket of water. His firework had set the shed on fire.

But luckily, Biff and Chip had vanished.

Chapter 6

Biff and Chip returned safely with the key. Mortlock took everyone to a bright, welcoming room where there was a table, laden with food.

"Time to eat," said Mortlock. "Pizzas, samosas, lamb kebabs, salads, crusty bread. Can I offer you milk or fruit juice?"

Tyler ate as if he was starving. "I've never 'ad such a feast before," he said. He gave Mortlock a sideways look. "What sort of place is this?" he asked.

Mortlock explained that they were in a place that exists outside normal time.

"I don't get it," mumbled Tyler, with his mouth full of bread.

They spoke about the Virans, and Wilma told them that the ones they had met seemed like ordinary people.

"No, they were scary!" shuddered Wilf. "They made everything cold and dark."

"Ah!" Mortlock said. "They don't always give off coldness or darkness. They can appear to be quite normal. But they are not humans. Their aim is to bring about chaos."

"But why do they explode?" asked Kipper.

"They are made of dark energy. It's like electricity. But they must be stopped. Their energy must be captured."

"Yeah, but it's great watching 'em go bang," grinned Tyler.

"Come on," said Mortlock, jumping to his feet. "Now we have the key, the TimeWeb will work. We'll set it up in the Library."

Mortlock connected the parts of the
TimeWeb together and Biff put the key in
the lock and turned it.

The blue sapphire in the centre of the Hub
glowed. Then light began to grow out of it.
It rose up like a beautiful tree with millions
of fine, delicate branches.

Mortlock let out a sigh. "The TimeWeb," he said. "Now our work must begin."

Now what?

The TimeWeb is set up and running! So now what? What does Mortlock mean when he says, "Now our work must begin"?

Biff and Chip had to be careful not to be seen when they went forward in time. Why?

A boy from the past has joined them. Why has he come? And what does Tyler think about the Time Vault and his new friends?

Are the children looking forward to fighting the Virans or does the thought of it scare them?

What missions will the TimeWeb find? How many Viran attacks will it reveal and how will Mortlock train the children to deal with them?

Grab Time Runners next so you can start to find out! There isn't much time. So hurry!

Virans

What is a Viran?	
Pure 'dark' energy.	
Aims	
To destroy all that is good throughout history and so create a future of darkness.	

Skills
They turn themselves into human form to live among people.
Weapons
'Dark Cloud' – Virans create darkness to hide in, or to confuse others.
'Coldness' – Virans draw energy, especially from light. In its place, they leave an icy chill that saps all who feel it.
'Viran Mind Stare' – Victims muddle their speech, and become confused or forgetful.
Weaknesses
Giving off coldness or darkness when annoyed or disturbed.
Can a Viran be stopped?
In its raw state, Viran energy can never be destroyed ... but it can be trapped and contained.

A Fold in Time

Imagine time as a long piece of tape.
At one end is now and at the other end is some time in the future.

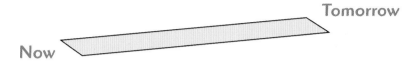

Tomorrow

Now

Imagine the same piece of tape has a fold in it. The tape still runs from now until tomorrow. But what would happen if you went into the fold? Time inside it would pass in a different way from real time.

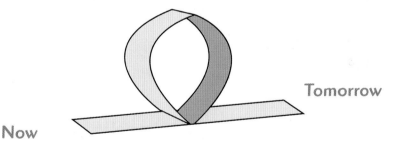

Tomorrow

Now

You would come out of the fold at almost the exact place that you went in. Within the fold, an hour, a week or even a month could have passed. But outside it, real time may only have moved on a few seconds.

Glossary

clutches *(page 19)* From the word 'clutch'. If you are in the clutches of someone, you are in their power. *"A good job too,"* said Wilma, *"or Kipper and Tyler might still be in the clutches of those Virans."*

crouched *(page 31)* Bent down. *Chip crouched behind the shed.*

intricate *(page 8)* With lots of delicate and complicated detail. *He was holding a small but highly intricate machine made of polished metal.*

laden *(page 33)* Heavily loaded or weighed down. *... there was a table, laden with food.*

merge *(page 7)* When two or more things join together. *Once again, the doors seemed to merge into one.*

samosa *(page 33)* A triangle–shaped pasty filled with meat or vegetables and fried in oil. *"Pizzas, samosas, lamb kebabs, salads, crusty bread."*

sapphire *(page 8)* A transparent blue crystal. A very precious gemstone. *In the very centre was a large sapphire of the deepest blue.*

Thesaurus: Another word for ...
crouch *(page 31)* squat, kneel, stoop, bob, bend down.

Have you read them all yet?

Level 11:

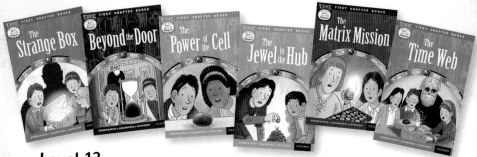

Level 12:

Time Runners

Tyler: His Story

A Jack and Three Queens

Mission Victory

The Enigma Plot

The Thief Who Stole Nothing

More great fiction from Oxford Children's:

About the Authors

Roderick Hunt MBE - creator of best-loved characters Biff, Chip, Kipper, Floppy and their friends. His first published stories were those he told his two sons at bedtime. Rod lives in Oxfordshire, in a house not unlike the house in the Magic Key adventures. In 2008, Roderick received an MBE for services to education, particularly literacy.

Roderick Hunt's son **David Hunt** was brought up on his father's stories and knows the world of Biff, Chip and Kipper intimately. His love of history and a good story has sparked many new ideas, resulting in the *Time Chronicles* series. David has had a successful career in the theatre, most recently working on scripts for Jude Law's *Hamlet* and *Henry V,* as well as Derek Jacobi's *Twelfth Night.*

Joint creator of the best-loved characters Biff, Chip, Kipper, Floppy and their friends, **Alex Brychta MBE** has brought each one to life with his fabulous illustrations, which are known and loved in many schools today. Following the Russian occupation of Czechoslovakia, Alex Brychta moved with his family from Prague to London. He studied graphic design and animation, before moving to the USA where he worked on animation for Sesame Street. Since then he has devoted many years of his career to *Oxford Reading Tree,* bringing detail, magic and humour to every story! In 2012 Alex received an MBE for services to children's literature.

Roderick Hunt and Alex Brychta won the prestigious Outstanding Achievement Award at the Education Resources Awards in 2009.

43

Levelling info for parents

What do the levels mean?

Read with Biff Chip & Kipper First Chapter Books have been designed by educational experts to help children develop as readers.

Each book is carefully levelled to allow children to make gradual progress and to feel confident and enjoy reading.

The Oxford Levels you will see on these books are used by teachers and are based on years of research in schools. Below is a summary of what each Oxford Level means, so that you can help your child to improve and enjoy their reading.

The books at Level 11 (Brown Book Band):

At this level, the sentence structures are becoming longer and more complex. The story plot may be more involved and there is a wider vocabulary. However, the proportion of unknown words used per paragraph/page is still carefully controlled to help build their reading stamina and allow children to read independently.

This level mostly covers characterisation through characters' actions and words rather than through description. The story may be organised in various ways, e.g. chronologically, thematically, sequentially, as relevant to the text type and subject.

The books at Level 12 (Grey Book Band):

At this level, the sentences are becoming more varied in structure and length. Though still straightforward, more inference may be required, e.g. in dialogue to work out who is speaking. Again, the story may be organised in various ways: chronologically, thematically, sequentially, etc., so that children can reflect on how the organisation helps the reader to understand the text.

The *Times Chronicles* books are also ideal for older children who feel less confident and need more practice in order to build stamina. The text is written to be age and ability appropriate, but also engaging, motivating and funny, making them a pleasure for children to read at this stage of their reading development.

OXFORD
UNIVERSITY PRESS

Great Clarendon Street, Oxford, OX2 6DP,
United Kingdom

Oxford University Press is a department of the University of Oxford.
It furthers the University's objective of excellence in research, scholarship,
and education by publishing worldwide. Oxford is a registered trade mark
of Oxford University Press in the UK and in certain other countries

Text © Roderick Hunt

Text written by David Hunt, based on the original characters
created by Roderick Hunt and Alex Brychta

Illustrations © Alex Brychta

The moral rights of the authors have been asserted

Database rights Oxford University Press (maker)

First published 2010
This edition published in 2015

British Library Cataloguing in Publication Data
Data available

978-0-19-273910-0

1 3 5 7 9 10 8 6 4 2

Paper used in the production of this book is a natural, recyclable product
made from wood grown in sustainable forests. The manufacturing process
conforms to the environmental regulations of the country of origin.

Printed in China

Acknowledgements: The publisher and authors would like to thank the following
for their permission to reproduce photographs and other copyright material:

P38tl claires/Shutterstock; **P38bl** Jose Ignacio Soto/Shutterstock;
P38-39 Hank Frentz/Shutterstock; **P38-39** Ragnarock/Shutterstock.

Book quiz answers

1 c

2 Floppy knocked the hourglass over, causing the bright specks to trickle down again.

3 Their house on New Year's Eve in the future.